HELPFUL PEOPLE

FIREFIGHTER

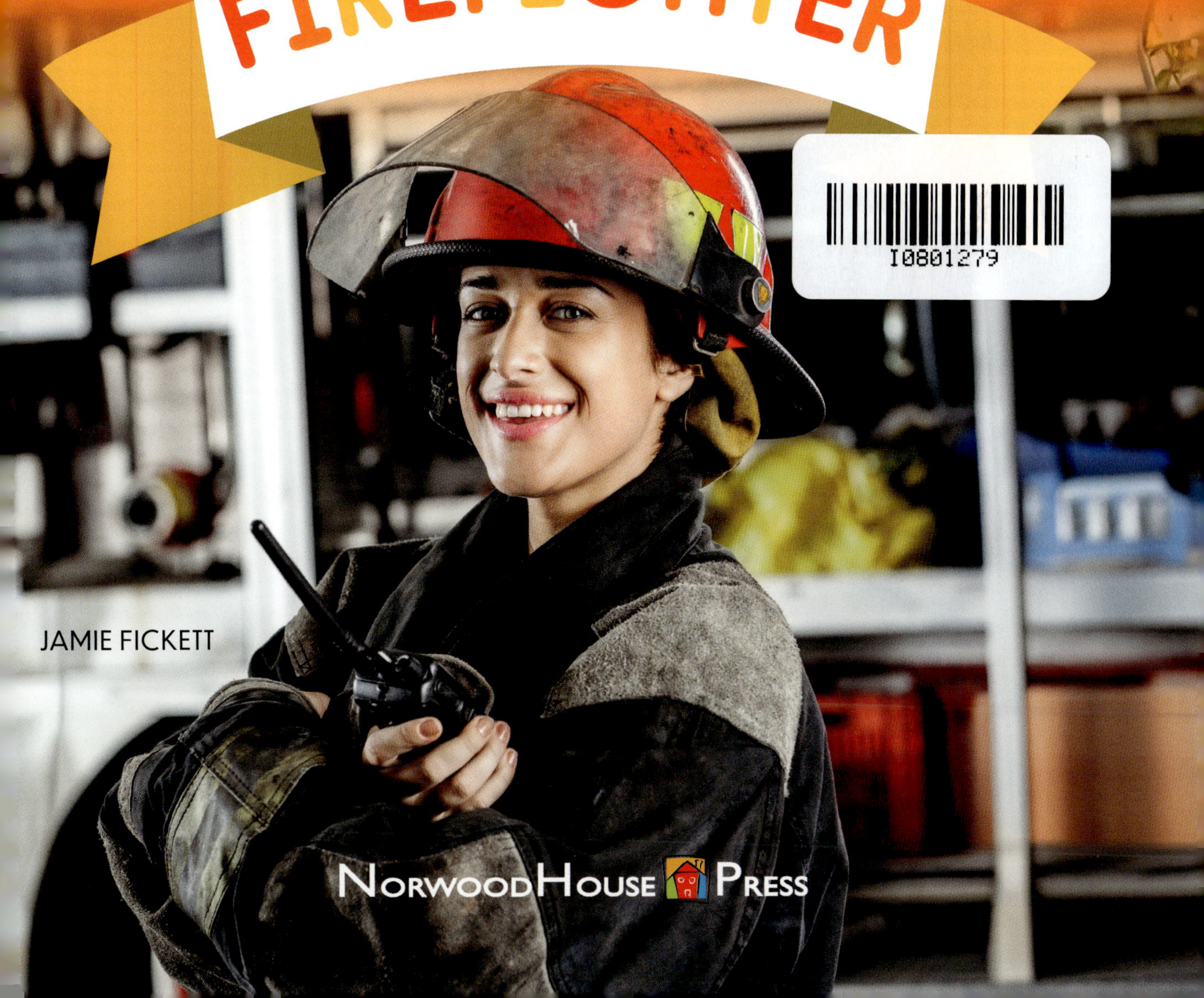

JAMIE FICKETT

NorwoodHouse Press

Library of Congress Cataloging-in-Publication Data:

Names: Fickett, Jamie.
Title: Firefighter / Jamie Fickett.
Description: Buffalo, NY : Norwood House Press, 2025. | Series: Helpful people | Includes glossary and index.
Identifiers: ISBN 9781684503018 (pbk.) | ISBN 9781684503025 (library bound) | ISBN 9781684503032 (ebook)
Subjects: LCSH: Fire fighters--Juvenile literature. | Fire extinction--Juvenile literature.
Classification: LCC TH9148.F535 2025 | DDC 363.37092--dc23

Published in 2025 by
Norwood House Press
2544 Clinton Street
Buffalo, NY 14224

Designer: Ocean Books
Editor: Kim Thompson

Photo credits: Cover, p. 1 Tyler Olson/Shutterstock.com; p. 5 Standret/Shutterstock.com; p. 6 Gorodenkoff/Shutterstock.com; p. 7 LukeOnTheRoad/Shutterstock.com; p. 9 wavebreakmedia/Shutterstock.com; p. 11 FXQuadro/Shutterstock.com; p. 12-13 Tyler Olson/Shutterstock.com; p. 13 FrameAngel/Shutterstock.com; p. 15 Colloidial/Shutterstock.com; p. 16-17 Teerapong mahawan/Shutterstock.com; p. 19 Kzenon/Shutterstock.com; p. 21 lovelyday12/Shutterstock.com

Printed in the United States of America

CPSIA compliance information: Batch #CW25NHP: For further information contact Norwood House Press at 1-800-237-9932.

TABLE OF CONTENTS

WHAT IS A FIREFIGHTER?

Firefighters are important helpers in our **community**. Their main job is to put out fires in houses, schools, and other buildings. They work fast to stop the fire from spreading.

19
22

Firefighters also rescue people who are trapped. If people are stuck in a car after an accident, firefighters can help.

Firefighters help during **natural disasters** like floods or earthquakes. They help people get to a safe place.

Firefighters can teach us how to be safe. They tell us what to do if we see a fire or smell smoke.

MATH

WHAT DOES A FIREFIGHTER WEAR?

Firefighters wear thick coats and pants. Their clothes have bright colors and shiny stripes so that people can see them in the dark and through the smoke.

Hard helmets **protect** firefighters from falling things. The helmets have special shields that cover the face.

Firefighters wear strong boots to protect their feet from sharp objects and hot ground. The boots are **waterproof**, so their feet stay dry.

Firefighters wear gloves so that their hands do not get cut or burned. The gloves are strong, but they are not stiff. Firefighters can still move their fingers to use their **tools**.

WHAT TOOLS DOES A FIREFIGHTER USE?

A fire truck carries hoses, water, and many other tools. Ladders on the truck help firefighters reach high places to rescue people.

Firefighters use hoses to spray water on the fire. The hoses attach to the fire truck or to fire hydrants.

Axes break through doors and windows. Then, firefighters can enter burning buildings to rescue people and pets.

HOW DO YOU BECOME A FIREFIGHTER?

Firefighters go to the **fire academy** to learn how to put out fires safely. They also learn how to help people in **emergencies**.

After the fire academy, firefighters take a test. If they pass the test, they can start working at a fire station.

Good firefighters are very **brave**. They are strong enough to carry heavy hoses and climb ladders quickly. They are quick thinkers during emergencies. They keep us safe.

GLOSSARY

brave (brave): having the courage to do dangerous or risky things

community (kuh-MYOO-ni-tee): a social group of any size whose members live together, have a common government, and often share the same culture or history

emergencies (i-MUR-juhn-seez): sudden and dangerous situations that require immediate action

fire academy (fire uh-KAD-uh-mee): a school or college that provides special instruction and training for firefighters

natural disasters (NACH-ur-uhl di-ZAS-turz): sudden and terrible events in nature that cause damage, suffering, and loss of life

protect (pruh-TEKT): to guard and keep safe from harm, attack, injury, or danger

tools (toolz): pieces of equipment that you use to do a job; things that help you reach a goal

waterproof (WAW-tur-proof): made of a special material, such as rubber, that does not let water through

THINKING QUESTIONS

1. What is the job of a firefighter?
2. Why does a firefighter wear special boots?
3. How is a firefighter helpful to the community?
4. What are the characteristics of a good firefighter?
5. Would you like to become a firefighter? Why or why not?

INDEX

ABOUT THE AUTHOR

Jamie Fickett lives on Long Island, New York, where he grew up. Every Saturday he enjoys going to the Bronx Zoo and seeing the rhinos from the Wild Asia Monorail. Rhinoceroses have been his favorite animal ever since he was eight and received the nickname Rhino while playing catcher in Little League baseball.